BY THE LIGHT OF THE SEA

JEAN-LOUP DARAUX

EN PASSANT PAR LA DEMEURE

BY THE LIGHT OF THE SEA

Photographs by Mario Ciampi

verbavolant

To my father

« *Faire longuement rêver ceux qui ordinairement n'ont pas de songes et plonger dans l'actualité ceux dans l'esprit desquels prévalent les jeux perdus du sommeil.* »

— René Char
Recherche de la base et du sommet

Contents

Introduction

BY THE LIGHT OF THE SEA

By the light of the sea, the light of the Mediterranean… after I left the southwest where I was born, it was here that I dipped my brush in the light and the sun of the Mediterranean. It was here where I "created" these homes that I would like to describe to you, where I would like to take you, to let you wander from one to another in no special order, from one picture to the next, without any purpose other than sharing these places with you, places to relax and feel at ease, comfortably content. Placid contentment, silence and space, in gentle soft light, filtered by the lowered shades of my "studio-home". Content to be on the beach, feet in the water, head and heart "by the light of the sea" in Anny's house where the slightest breeze fills the curtains like a sail, where the houses almost seem to cast off to sea from their moorings. And last of all, the contentment of recalling happy memories and carefree parties in the *cabanon* nestled in the sand, decorated with the multicoloured dreams of late summer, released after a long siesta. Here is also elsewhere. The exotic is at home here.

With this book, let me take you to this region of the Mediterranean, so fertile that anything will flourish… flowers and talent, art, poetry and films, love and new friendships. Since the time of ancient Greece, and even earlier, but still today, this is a place where one has a sense of freedom, free to be oneself, to create, free to love but also to live, quite simply, to be content, to free-wheel, without worrying about too much perfection. It is here that I nurtured my dreams and my passion for others. Here I wrote my poetry in the not quite perfect tense, this style, both sincere and casual, often out of step… which I have made my own. It is here that I have arranged and furnished homes for others and for those close to me, homes which all have one thing in common, a mixture of aspiration, pleasure and savoir-faire. There are some you will not see and with which I have lost contact. And there are those that I am happy to share with you… those houses which because of lasting friendship or because I live in them, still "belong" to me. And to help you let go completely, to help you give free rein to your imagination, I have laid out a table of contents—of material things—which have never been that well defined, a crossroads of different styles and origins, a list like the poem by Jacques Prevert, "one stone, two houses, three ruins, twelve oysters and one lemon, one door and one door mat… one flower garden". I will show you my materials from A to Z… from alabaster to zinc, including wood, iron, paper, paint… materials both natural and processed, left free or tamed… just as I have learned to contemplate them, use them and come to love them.

Throughout the book, here and there, you will come across my paintings and my sculptures. I have placed them carefully as clues to the secrets hidden between these pages as you read. It makes no difference whether you turn the pages one by one following the chosen order, or fly from one photo to another. In my houses, and all through this region, every path leads to a new surprise. My only aim is the pleasure you may find in letting your mind wander for a moment to discover some small surprise as you come across it. Just as it happened to me the other morning when, a few yards from my home, I found that someone had written "*La vie est belle*" on the wall of the old village wash house. How wonderful to imagine that those words had been written by Pierrot "by the light of the sea".

« Ceux qui campent chaque jour plus loin
du lieu de leur naissance, ceux qui tirent chaque jour
leur barque sur d'autre rives savent mieux chaque jour
le cour des choses illisibles. »

— Saint-John Perse
Neiges, IV. Exil. Poésie.

My paintings
colour my world

My mother had a lovely expression "making things comes easily to you". Painting, repairing, gluing, welding, putting together, sculpting, and even "rhyming" as I like to call it; it seems to me that I have loved doing these things all my life. One day a very long time ago, somebody told me that art was etched in the lines of my hand. In short all my life, over the years, I have collected, painted, sculpted... until one day I found that I desperately needed a place to keep the exuberant results of all this artistic work. And I found it, this place, I am not sure whether by accident or because it brought back the nostalgia of the toy garage I had when I was small, and used to "play cars".

My studio, and now my home as well, is actually an old Packard garage from the days before the War. And this garage has more than simple familiarities: like my toy garage it has the same two big stories, the same access ramp, same two office floors, same terrace roof, and even the wide openings are identical and the vast expanses without columns. The only one difference—it is not on a small scale. Elevated as well as underground, it spreads out to create surprising spaces as well as more intimate areas, perfect for living and working, family life and inviting a few friends. At the same time, it makes me think of an island that one can cross from one end to the other without any form of barrier, from one shore to the other, we have not cast an anchor, but we have found the perfect parking spot in this place which we continue to call "The Garage". Once we found the right place, we needed to make it habitable. Imagination ran riot. The only thing we were sure of was that we were sure of nothing. None of the conventional criteria worked here. What an opportunity.

Since I am not attracted to minimalist austerity, I played around with contrasts and harmony, "unadjusting" them. The metamorphosis was radical. I mixed contemporary with antique, languid serene colours with others that were audacious, light refined materials with the raw, wood and concrete, mosaics and metal. And of course I filled it with objects, selected for their unlimited poetry. Last of all my paintings, hung everywhere, are like a succession of "open sesames" leading to the internal spaces. At last, they had a home!

Here everyone immediately finds their own personal space. During the renovation work, the plumber parked in the spot which has become my bedroom. The electrician preferred the body repair shop, which is now dedicated to preparing haute cuisine. And those who live here today enjoy different views and perspectives from floor to floor, floating off, each one to his own personal dream world. Peaceful contentment has crept in, up the old access ramp. Sometimes I like to think that this serenity has also chosen to park itself in our "Garage".

Almodóvar heroines?
Reminders of the Feria
painted on torn posters.

Mirrors with no reflection and white slipcovers. Memories of *The Intruder* by Visconti.

Where angels fear to tread.

Wooden horses, simply because they are made
of wood... seem to come from a bygone age.
Nothing remains but the soul deep within...
I have been collecting horses for years.
They are scattered all through the house.

The Marquis' carriage awaits.

Chercher midi à cinq heures, moins cinq.

C'est un poème des Fleurs du Mal qui m'a inspiré ce tableau :
« (…) Tu trouveras au bout de deux beaux seins
bien lourds, deux larges médailles de bronze,
Et, sous un ventre uni, doux comme du velours,(…) »
— Charles Baudelaire *Les promesses d'un visage*

Dinner is ready!

« *Puisse toujours durer une si grande joie.* »
— Jean Cocteau

A bit of sun for
"the smallest rooms"
in the house

Toward the terrace and bedrooms.

To the devil with avarice, there were so many antennas on the surrounding rooftops I added another.

Down to the studio.

Dentelles larges
20 à 30 cm
pr pentes de fête des
petits autels
et pour rochets

I love to sculpt large birds and hang them from the ceiling to watch them in constant motion.

and a partridge here, a
sparrow there...

... followed by the cavalry...

"The Hunt"

« *En attendant pour voir plus loin*
Les yeux grands ouverts, sous le vent de ses mains,
Elle imagine que l'horizon a pour elle dénoué sa ceinture. »

— Paul Éluard

La grande maison inhabitable Répétitions

Nothing but
blue skies do i see...

Anny, my prodigious friend, eternally travelling the world on business, ever in perpetual motion, wanted a house "with its feet in the water" where she could finally let go and relax. Coincidence sometimes works in our favour. A visit to where she had lived as a child… and she found what she had been searching for. But the first time I saw the house, I found it decidedly unattractive, with its pointed roof, longer on one side than the other. I might as well be honest, at first glance it looked like a cheap cardboard Christmas crib stuck on the edge of a beach. What was it doing there? This crib, looking as if it had been placed on a skiff, on this piece of rock that seemed to float while sitting deep in the water, completely surrounded by a universe of sea and sky… infinite shades of blue changing with each hour. Those were my immediate thoughts before I even began to imagine what I could do to improve it.

The work started and it was a long job. The splendour of endless sea and sky—sometimes blending and obscuring the horizon—surrounding the house left no other choice but strict simplicity. But simplicity is demanding, and creating the minimum does not mean doing as little as possible. Perhaps it means remaining with only what is strictly necessary, a small detail that could not exist in any other place creating a surprise that leads to yet another detail?

So we began to patiently take over Anny's house, little by little, so that calmly, gently and without havoc, the accents of the Mediterranean from Greece, Morocco, Italy and Spain blended softly together, murmuring of travels, friendships made, recollections, memories and hopeful expectations. Giono wrote, "not a millimetre of the world is without its own flavour" and that is what we tried to achieve. Nothing missing: light, plain, pure, practical elegant, discrete. This is a house full of flavour. Right down to the materials… down to the traces left here and there by the sun and the sea.

Whenever I am there, a guest in this quietly discrete house hidden from view by its grey shutters… in this house which seems to want to live incognito, and can only be photographed from the sea, when I lie relaxed in a deck chair idly watching the boats just as lazily rocking on the water, filtered by this translucent light, I seem to hear, like the echo from a shell pressed to your ear, the fleeting whisper of freedom caress my cheek.

Be careful of sunburn, lobster-red!

A weekend in Rome, inspired this painting. I remember while you were riding your bikes in the gardens of the Villa Borghese, I lay on a bench and contemplated the scraps of bright blue sky showing through the branches of an umbrella pine. In Rome, the sky is still blue even at night. "Week-end in Rome… for the *dolce far'niente*… to smile again… weekend in Rome… those nights, those nights" Etienne Daho still sings these words.

I painted this bowl with gold fish
thinking of the song by Françoise Hardy:
"I put a crab in the bowl
where my goldfish were looking bored (…)
and with his lopsided walk
he changed the course of time (…)"

We could have brought back a bottle of ouzo, but we decided on these coloured chairs discovered on a terrace in Mykonos.

The tables are separated or put together according to the number of guests and the evenings are brightened by multicoloured lights.

"Correspondence"

A Moroccan door as a headboard,
a souvenir.

Poème pour une statue

C'est sans regret et sans vergogne
Qu'un jour au bras d'un antiquaire
J'ai quitté ma natale Bourgogne
Et ce pour aller voir la mer.
Bien sûr je n'ai pas de visage
Je pourrais être Marie ou Sainte Anne
Si vous voulez connaître mon âge
Pas de doute je suis bien romane.
Regardez comme je suis belle
Il y a sur ma robe encore
quelques restes de bleu, un peu d'or
Mais il est une chose sûre
Ça ne cache en rien mes blessures.
C'est bien parce que j'ai souffert
Que lorsque vous irez prier
Tous les bons chemins je connais
Pour faire monter depuis la terre
Tout là-haut vers le ciel vos prières.

1er janvier 2007

Gift for the first of the year.

This life preserver was cast ashore here, like a bottle with a message on the sand.

Milky white, stone like alabaster.

Candles electrify the way up the stairs.

And steps
that go down into
an endless sea.

The swimming pool,
a pool of sea water in the rocks.

« … et si vous ouvrez la barrière qu'un enfant briserait, vous entrez sans gravir
ni descendre une marche, vous entrez de plain-pied dans la mer. »

— Colette

La Treille muscate. Prisons et paradis.

THE WHOLE WORLD
ON MY DOORSTEP

We had dreamed about it for years and we had searched for it for months, pacing up and down the beaches from Pampelonne to Ramatuelle, in one direction, then the other… and back again. It had to be right on the water's edge, and it had to have this, and had to be like that… until one day we found it. It had been thrown up quickly a few years before for a lifeguard. It was in the rushes, on the sand, facing the water. There was nothing special about it. Except that it was there… and it was just what we wanted. You always end up finding what belongs to you. That was twenty-seven years ago. Time flies!

Out of this shelter we built a do-it-yourself paradise, rainbow-coloured, inspired by paintings by an artist from the Philippines, always dressed in gypsy skirts, and who considered herself the local Frida Kahlo. Each time I went to the Philippines for work I brought back some of her canvases… glimpses of another place, brightly coloured fun, naïf and filled with sun. From these paintings we gleaned the colours to decorate our fifty square metres on the sand at the water's edge. With huge brush-strokes, we painted an exhilarating backdrop canvas in Gitane cigarette packet blue, theatre curtain red, sunshine yellow… To the non-stop background music of Abba's *Dancing Queen*, we painted every surface with bright colours, inside and out, down to the furniture and dishes we designed ourselves and even the letter box has a title—inspired by the cover of a Spanish magazine—that seemed to have been created especially for this little corner of paradise, *La vida en horizontal*.

Since that moment we have not touched a thing. With only a few bits and pieces, the *cabanon* gave the impression that it included every exotic style on the planet. The whole world on our doorstep. It was as if this wild explosion of colour attracted all that was joyful and carefree… and little by little, silently, it spread contagiously, to include the landscape and all that surrounded it. For almost thirty years we have not changed anything (except for a few gas bottles for the cooker) That is the reason why, alongside the "Garage" and Anny's beach home, I wanted to include this *cabanon*. It is a little out of step, like a slightly cheeky desert at the end of a formal dinner. Because we are urged on all sides to constantly improve, modernise, update, and follow the latest fashions and trends (and I should know!) Perhaps we too often forget that only the immobility of certain things and places will allow time in constant motion to stop and leave a trace of its existence. This is the lesson we have taken from our "marshmallow" *cabanon*. In this small haven, we have been made fully aware of the need to observe life as it passes by. Fleeting and fragile[*].

[*] *This has proved true, because soon our little* cabanon *will be nothing more than a memory, a few pictures preserved in this book and our photo albums. A building project will soon erase it from the landscape, but certainly not from our hearts.*

Green screen.

Good-sized fish.
Found in a fish shop
in Marseilles.

The momentum carried to a design for a chair.

No, it is not a gold fish in a bowl.

and who is that?

Cats love to sit in boxes…

... and on young girls' laps.

This house is full of things that are of no use at all. The hardest thing when trying to explain to friends who want to bring you "something practical" as a gift is that you really do prefer to live here without a vegetable peeler or a potato masher, etc.

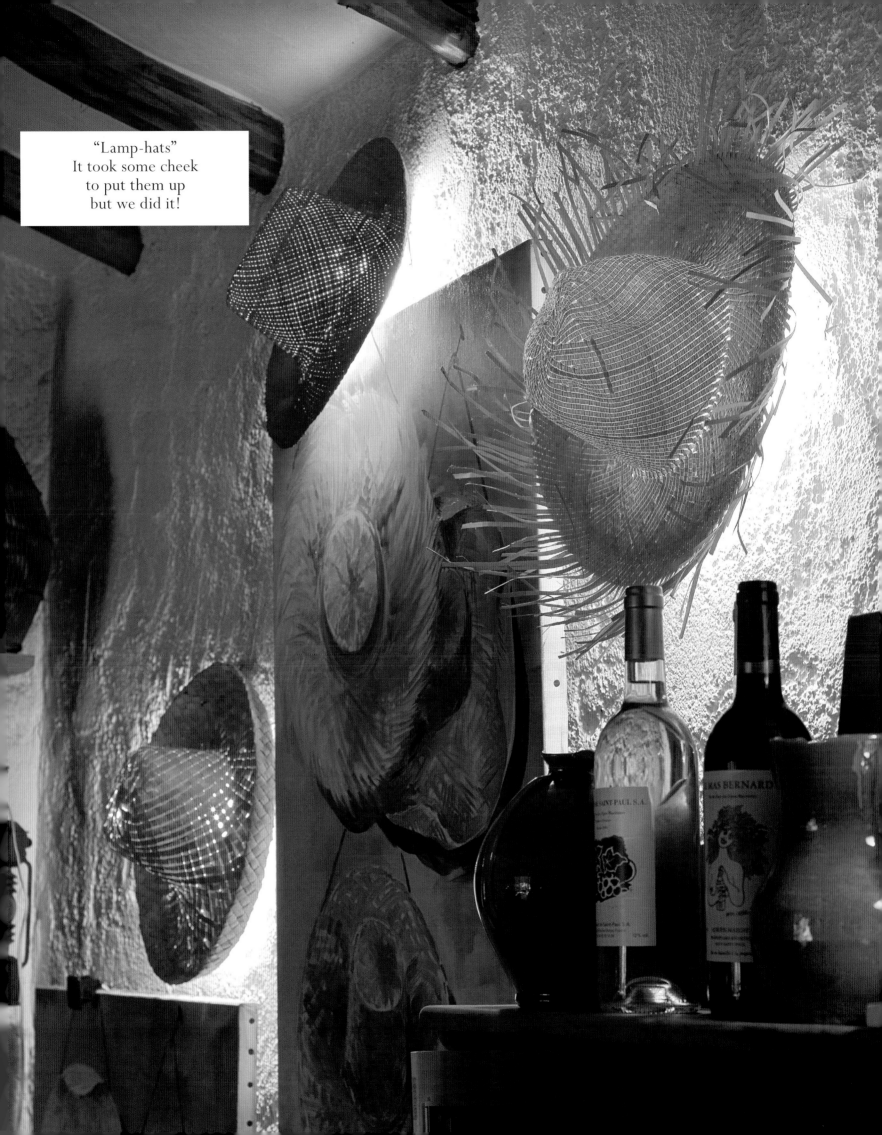

"Lamp-hats"
It took some cheek
to put them up
but we did it!

Petit discours au dessert pour un anniversaire

Nous faisons trois minutes de pause
Pour les anniversaires au dessert je cause
J'aurais pu vous le faire en prose
Qu'à cela ne tienne en vers j'ose.

Quand sous la treille on se repose
Que les cigales chantent et pour cause
Que de vin de Rasque on dispose
De boire un coup je vous propose.

Car comme les légumes et les roses
Eh bien! l'amitié ça s'arrose.
Et quand on aime pas question de dose
Allons-y donc jusqu'à la cirrhose!

juin 2008

swing

Nothing but pieces of
driftwood for this work of art.

MATERIAL THINGS

This is not an overstatement, but I feel that had a vocation for materials just as others have a religious calling. I love them all, wood, metal, stone, paper, fabrics… all of them, without exception and without preference. We are constantly surprised by the beauty. I love wood in every shape and form. I am always excited when I find a piece of driftwood on the beach, wood that has travelled from who knows where, brought in by the waves and cast ashore "sanded", and beautifully perfect in its simplicity. I still find myself stopping in my tracks in Camargue confronted by railway sleepers, stuck in the ground like totem poles, wound with barbed wire, to form an enclosure for the bulls. Never completely vertical, standing steadfast in the middle of the marshes… perches for birds, accidental sculptures. Stark and wonderful! And I love to hunt for those old wooden statues, survivors of centuries past, and a little mutilated by the years, perhaps armless, sometimes without legs or a face, but which, even fragmented, seem intent on telling their history. I am fascinated by wood, not simply the piece of wood used to carve a flute, but the wood of old doors, or recycled shutters that we use on work sites. Split and fractured, sculpted by the weather, sometimes still with a bit of colour, when they are set in place because of their unique appearance, they seem to thank use for letting them continue to serve a purpose. What can I say about wood? The variety of species, the fragrance of cedar that pervades the dressing rooms we build, age-old oak that creaks elegantly in re-laid parquets and panelling, blond mahogany for bookshelves straight from English gentlemen's clubs, and palissander with its beautiful fine veining. There is not one species I do not love.

Time has simplified the contour and smoothed the profile. A new piece of art has been created. Every bit as beautiful.

A ceiling made of branches.
Light and shade
in oblique lines.

Other birds on a branch,
like a large weather vane.

I love iron too, the iron used to build antique greenhouses, or hand rails, balconies and furniture… You can use it to draw on sheet metal and it stands out, a charcoal line, black, clear, solid, permanent! I love iron because it lies between the flame and the anvil, because it comes down to us from the beginning of time. For this alone, it deserves a place of its own. How can Roland's sword Durandal not spring to mind whenever I go into a working forge… Time seems to stand still. I love to work iron myself, I love welding, forging, putting together all sorts of pieces to create giant birds or elongated figures. I love mixing iron with wood. Addictive! How can I not love the haphazard conglomeration assembled on this door, pieces of sheet metal of all shapes and sizes welded together at random, and recovered to become the back door to the "Garage"? And again, how can one not be enchanted by the successive repairs on this very old watering can that I have had for so many years? I look at them and see unexpected works of art, accidents of fortune.

When I paint, instead of blank canvas, I prefer the huge sheets of raw linen, enormous, often patched, that are spread under olive trees for the harvest. They still keep the traces of the harvest season. They are almost tanned like leather, and I love to discover on the surface, those initial lines that will eventually become a part of my work. I love cement bags as well; the incredible quality of the paper, so resistant and yet so porous that it bleaches every colour into a watercolour wash. And posters, torn down from walls at nightfall; I love to work on them, back side, right side, and even before I start… the layers glued on top of one another, some letters here, a piece of a face there … tell me the beginning of the story I will paint. These vignettes that I place in my work, pieces of old manuscripts with illegible spidery writing, hieroglyphs, messages from another moment in time, … hidden meanings, unpredictable treasure hunts.

It is true, I have a weak spot for profusion, but I am just as happy before the white plaster of an empty room that we are about to decorate… like a musical score on which we can play any range of colour in harmony. We play, we grope about, one colour after another, placing one next to another, one without the other, and why not yet another? Why not come back to the first one we chose, but stronger, or softer, or warmer, touches of colour, just a try… or carefully calculated? And so the melody is composed a piece at a time, on the walls, the ceilings, on the panelling, the cornices and the mouldings… with a few tones of well-tuned colour.

Let us not forget marble and stone. Whether its name is Ampilly, Buxy, Langres, Aurore, Chanteuil, Corton, or Calacata… they are noble names fit for a duchess. They can be hard or tender, light or cold. They can be milky white, transparent or the deepest black. They come from every corner of the world, India, China, Italy, Bourgogne and sometimes even from nearby, close to the house we are decorating. They all hold a secret. Each one holds a surprise in the heart of each block or slab. Split open, suddenly they reveal shells, veins, mica. I love to discover these messages of former lives, thousands of years old. So we transform it into mosaic flooring, bench tops, even complex work, carving baths and basins from a single block, sometimes over half a ton in weight. And like a duchess, stone and marble like to be recognised for their quality; we must be able to choose just the right finish for the location for which they are destined. Timeless, vibrant, secret, mysterious, proud… but for those who know how to caress the smooth surface, little by little it will loose its coolness and will never cease to amaze.

Fabric or paint, stone, wood or iron… there is no material I do not love. Each one has a story to tell, a history, and the source of a hidden world that seeks nothing more than to be contemplated, preferably with the eyes of a child, unrestricted and still able to see the magic.

Concrete cut up like stone flagging.

First published in 2008 by

Verba Volant Ltd.
Pellipar House, First Floor
9 Cloak Lane
London EC4R 2RU

By the Light of the Sea was created and produced by Verba Volant Ltd.

verbavolant

e-mail: info@verbavolantbooks.com
website: www.verbavolantbooks.com

ISBN-10: 1-905216-20-3
ISBN-13: 978-1-905216-20-8

Text: Jean-Loup Daraux
e-mail: jeanloupdaraux@wanadoo.fr

Translated from the French by Katy Hannan

Printed in China by Sing Cheong Printing Co. Ltd.

A recovered municipal panel:
an artwork — Thank you chance!